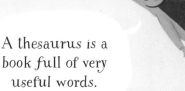

A thesaurus is a book full of very useful words.

USBORNE
Big Picture
THESAURUS

Written by
Rosie Hore

Illustrated by
Rachael Saunders

Designed by
Emily Barden

In this book, you'll find lists of words with similar meanings to help you find new words to use.

You'll also find opposites...

...and ways of describing things precisely. Instead of walk, try...

daring, bold, courageous

bad
evil
villainous

good
lovely
nice

tiptoe, sneak, creep

Contents

See how many times you can spot us in this book.

wash clean scrub

TWEET

yellow
lemon gold

red
crimson scarlet
ruby tomato

WHIZZ journey, trip, outing

HIKING TRAIL

CARAVAN PARK

BAA

hike, trek, ramble

tall high towering

MMM

yummy tasty delicious

swell, churn, froth

leafy lush

windy gusty breezy

sandy, dusty, dry

SNORT

Keep on going!

Home and family

Where do you live?
house
cottage
bungalow
flat
apartment
mobile home
houseboat
mansion

Homes can be...
big
grand
splendid
or...
small
cosy
comfortable
snug

Houses can have...
a roof
an upstairs
a downstairs
floors
windows
a basement
a front door
a back door
a garden

Playroom

toys
games
activities

cuddle
hug
embrace

HMM

GIGGLE

Bedroom

asleep
dozing

wake up
get up

DRING DRING

untidy
messy
chaotic

Bathroom

toilet
loo
lavatory

Kitchen

mop, wipe

slip
trip

clean
tidy
put away

cook
prepare
make

Living room
lounge
sitting room

nap
snooze

curtains
drapes

throw away
get rid of
discard
chuck out

meeow

sweep, brush

Why is it always me who takes out the rubbish?

You've got a letter, a packet, a parcel *and* a package today.

RUFF

4

Attic
dusty
grubby
musty

dingy
dim
dark

wash
scrub

soapy
foamy

sofa
settee
couch

SNORE

shed
store
outhouse

search
look for
hunt

Who do you
live with?

family
relations
relatives

grandparents

grandpa
grandad
grandfather
grandpop

grandma
granny
grandmother
nanny
gran

parents

mother
mum
mummy
ma
mama
mom

father
dad
daddy
pa
papa
pop

children

uncle

aunt

niece

nephew

cousins

pet

siblings
brothers and sisters
sons and daughters

We have
lots of *family*
members.

Our *family*
is small.

eldest
oldest
biggest

twins

youngest
littlest

babies
litter
brood

5

Getting around

You can go on a...
journey
trip
outing
excursion
ride
voyage
tour

car

What a lovely day for a drive.

Buy your tickets on board.

bus

van

Planes... fly, take off
WHOOSH
aeroplane

Journeys can be...
short *or* long
quick *or* slow
bumpy *or* smooth
one-way *or* return
on time *or* delayed
planned *or* surprise

baggage
cases
luggage

overtake, go past

motorbike, motorcycle

speed up
accelerate

delivery bike
moped

Cars have...
wheels
tyres
an engine
a windscreen
seat belts
a bonnet
headlights
front seats
back seats
a steering wheel
a boot
bumpers
brakes

BANG!
crash
accident
collision
smash
BOOM!

PETROL STATION
Pay here!

petrol, fuel, gas, gasoline, diesel

RELIABLE REMOVALS

Trucks and lorries...
carry
transport
deliver

Not so fast!

hiss

broken down

Boats might...
float, drift, cruise, steam

pedalo

splash

rowing boat

VAROOM

motor boat

Measuring and investigating

What size?

huge, gigantic, enormous

big
large

small
little
mini

tiny
minute
miniscule

width

wider
broader

narrower
thinner

taller

height

shorter

length

longer

shorter

getting bigger
growing
expanding
enlarging
swelling

getting smaller
shrinking
decreasing
reducing
dwindling

PUFF

How heavy?

balanced, equal, same

unbalanced

heavy
weighty

light
lightweight

BOB

float

sink

How far?

distance, extent, range

near
close
nearby

far
distant
far away

How many?

count
add up
tally
total

1 2 3 4 5 6 7 8 9 10

amount
quantity
number

several
many
lots
loads

few
hardly any
not many
a couple

adding

subtracting
taking away

double

half

dividing
sharing
splitting

part
fraction
segment
section
piece

whole
complete

What is it made of?

plastic

rubber

metal

stone

glass

wood

paper

cloth

clay

What does it feel like?

hard *or* soft
rough *or* smooth
sharp *or* rounded
stiff *or* stretchy
firm *or* squashy

fluffy

Comparisons

shallow

deep

deeper

empty

full
filled

overflowing

matching
identical

similar
alike

different
clashing

Your body

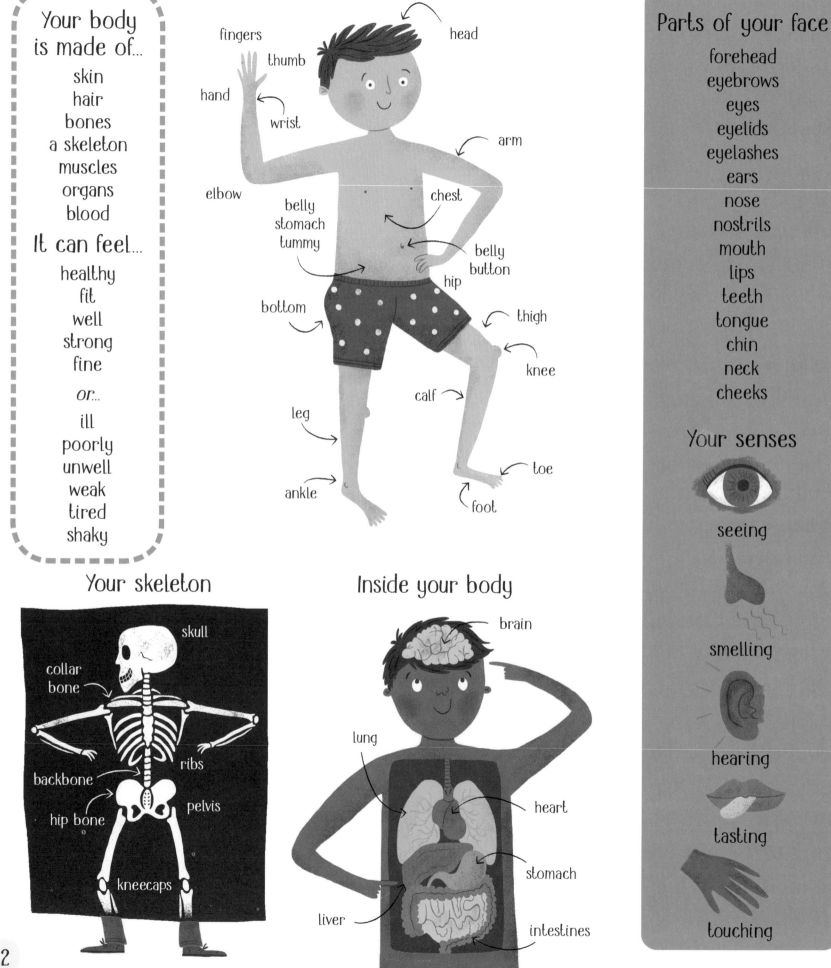

Your body is made of...
- skin
- hair
- bones
- a skeleton
- muscles
- organs
- blood

It can feel...
- healthy
- fit
- well
- strong
- fine

or...
- ill
- poorly
- unwell
- weak
- tired
- shaky

fingers
thumb
hand
wrist
elbow
head
arm
belly
stomach
tummy
chest
belly button
hip
thigh
bottom
knee
calf
leg
ankle
toe
foot

Your skeleton

skull
collar bone
backbone
hip bone
ribs
pelvis
kneecaps

Inside your body

brain
lung
heart
liver
stomach
intestines

Parts of your face
- forehead
- eyebrows
- eyes
- eyelids
- eyelashes
- ears
- nose
- nostrils
- mouth
- lips
- teeth
- tongue
- chin
- neck
- cheeks

Your senses

seeing

smelling

hearing

tasting

touching

12

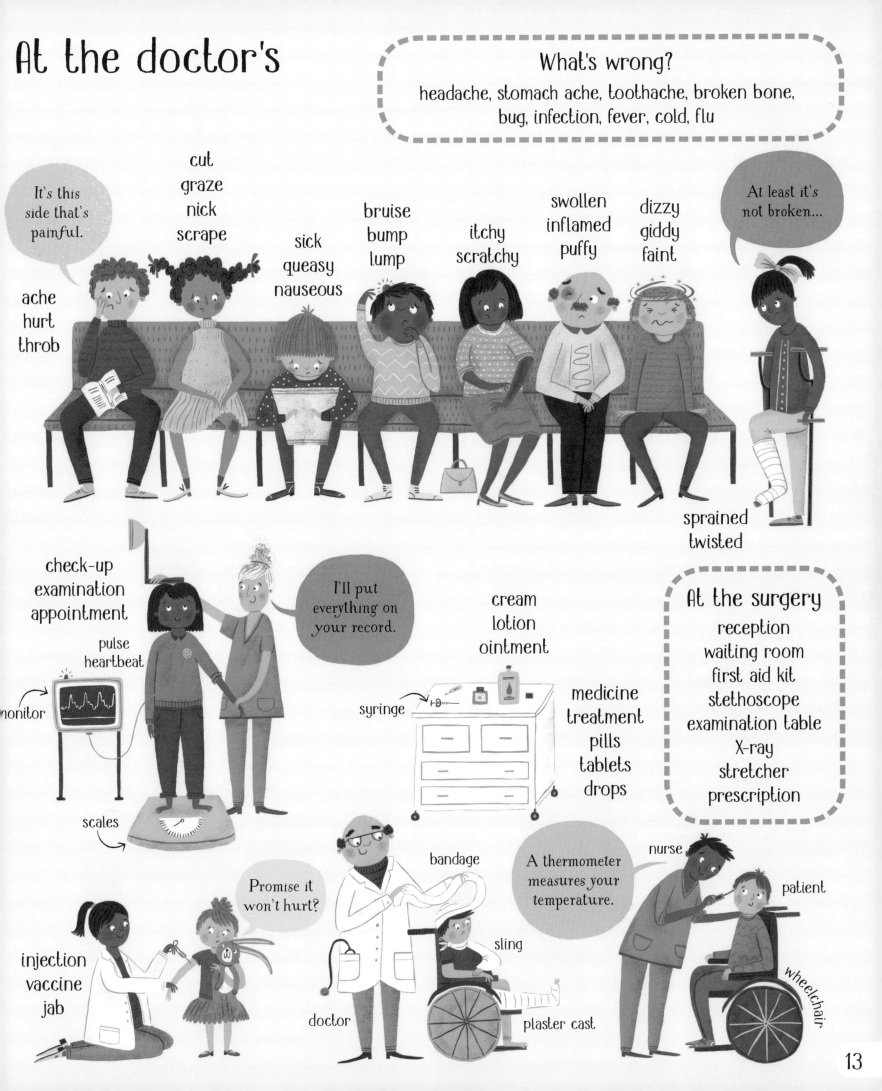

Describing people

People can look...
- pretty
- beautiful
- handsome
- attractive
- glamorous
- fashionable
- stylish
- cool
- smart
- shabby
- scruffy
- unusual
- unique
- individual

tall
lanky

short
little
petite

fat
stout
stocky

thin
skinny
slim

Ha ha, I look so gangly!

I remember being in the circus!

bald

SPIN   SPIN

freckles

twiddle

baby
toddler

child
kid

teenager
young person

adult
grown-up

old
elderly

Hair can be...
- long
- cropped
- curly
- frizzy
- straight
- wavy
- wiry
- tangled
- glossy

Hair colours

blonde
fair

black
dark

brown
brunette

red
ginger
auburn

grey
silvery

People can be...

helpful, lovely, kind, thoughtful, funny, witty, friendly, honest, talented, unkind, nosy, boring, annoying, selfish, lazy, mean, rude, greedy

chatty
talkative

or...

quiet
silent

That looks
far too
dangerous.

reckless
rash

or...

sensible
practical

silly
bizarre
odd
wacky
peculiar
quirky

or...

serious
stern
solemn

strong
muscular
beefy

or...

GASP

weak
puny
feeble

Whoops!

SPLAT

curtsey

graceful
elegant
poised

or...

clumsy
accident-prone
awkward

polite
well mannered
well behaved

or...

cheeky
mischievous
naughty

15

How are you feeling?

I'm feeling HAPPY!

happy
in a good mood
glad
joyful

whistle

cheerful
jolly
upbeat

When you're happy you...
smile
grin
beam
laugh
giggle
chuckle

Best day ever!

delighted
ecstatic

I'm feeling SAD.

sad
unhappy
low
gloomy
miserable

When you're unhappy you...
frown
cry
sob
moan
sulk

moody
grumpy
snappy

hurt
upset

devastated

I'm feeling SCARED.

scared
frightened
afraid

nibble

anxious
nervous
worried

terrified
petrified
fearful

When you're scared you...
scream
shriek
jump
shake
shiver

I'm feeling ANGRY.

angry
cross
grumpy
moody

ARRRRRRG

furious
livid
mad

When you're angry you...
scowl
shout
huff
yell
argue

You don't understand!

annoyed
frustrated

Animals

Animals can have...

a tail
paws
claws
prickles
horns
fangs
hooves
whiskers
antlers
quills
a trunk

GRRR
ROAR

wild
fierce
ferocious

crunch

rare
uncommon
endangered

Awesome! I've never seen a panda in real life before.

PAT
tame
obedient
WAG

sleepy
dozy
drowsy

Animals that only eat plants are called herbivores.

alert
attentive watchful
wary

camouflaged
disguised
hidden

Animals that only eat meat are called carnivores.

A crocodile's skin is...
scaly, dry, rough, bumpy

A bear's fur is...
soft
fuzzy
bushy
shaggy

lap

A panther's coat is...
shiny
silky
sleek

lick

Food and drink

Food can be...

raw
cooked
grilled
fried
baked
boiled
charred
steamed
barbecued
roasted

Ingredients
can be...

sliced
chopped
mashed
puréed

yummy
tasty
delicious

disgusting
revolting
nasty

GULP

sour
sharp
tart
tangy

MMMMM

munch

sweet
sugary
syrupy

salty
savoury
seasoned

smelly
stinky
strong

WHIFF
PONG

crumble

dry
stale

SPLASH

juicy
fresh
ripe

Vegetables

cucumber
melon
potato
broccoli
lemon
onion
salad
aubergines
date
chillies
carrot
cabbage

Fish

tuna
mussels
salmon
lobster
cod
prawns

Meat

steak
sausages
beef
bacon
lamb
chicken

In the fridge

butter
cream
milk
cheese
eggs
yoghurt

Fruit

grapes

apple

berries

orange

tomato

pomegranates

bananas

mild
bland
tasteless

spicy
peppery
hot

In the cupboard

rice

cereal

couscous

bread

noodles

pasta

beans

nuts

spices

herbs

pastries

oil

salt

pepper

flour

chocolate

sugar

tea

honey

water

coffee

juice

squash

CHOMP

crispy
crunchy

oily
greasy

Drinks

SLURP

fizzy
bubbly
sparkling

creamy
gooey
gloopy
sticky

Eating

You might be...
peckish
hungry
starving
ravenous
famished

or...
full
full up
satisfied

What do you
eat with?
knife
fork
spoon
chopsticks
your fingers

carton

bowl

plate

How do you eat?

nibble
bite
chew

or...

scoff
devour
munch
guzzle

Meals
breakfast
lunch
snack
tea
dinner
supper
feast

dessert
pudding

In a city

Cities can be...
busy
crowded
lively
hectic
buzzing
bustling
famous
expensive
diverse
sprawling

You can walk down...
roads
paths
pavements
alleys
avenues
streets
lanes
passages
boulevards
backstreets

Places to eat
restaurant
coffee shop
takeaway
café
food market

ice cream van

swimming pool

skyscraper

zip wire

playground

slide

fountain

library

park bench

SCHOOL

statue

BANK

train station

$

I'm late for work – again!

art gallery

THEATRE

canal

HOSPITAL

Will we see the mosque from the canal?

ambulance

SUPERMARKET

police station

car park

AIRPORT

terminal

aircraft ZOOOOM

runway

Buildings can be...

new
modern
contemporary

In the countryside

The countryside can be...
peaceful
quiet
tranquil
serene
scenic
rural
rustic

The scenery is...
beautiful
breathtaking
awe-inspiring
glorious
picturesque
impressive

summit
top
peak

mountain

wood
forest

Lots to do on the farm today.

tractor

field
meadow
pasture

wild flowers

hay bales

hedgerow

woof

sheep dog

farmer

gate

close
shut

fence

path, lane, track

Streams...
gurgle
babble
bubble
tinkle
trickle

Waterfalls...
gush
cascade
surge

Footpaths can be...
crooked
winding
twisting
curving
bumpy
uphill *or* downhill
grassy *or* bare
steep *or* flat

hike
wander
ramble

How many fish can you see?

Rivers...
flow
stream
rush

river bank

muddy
boggy
marshy

explore
investigate
discover

boulder

stone

pebbles

rock

By the sea

beach
seaside
coast
seashore
shore
bay

SOUVENIR SHOP

SHELL HOTEL

GUESTHOUSE
HOSTEL
BED AND BREAKFAST
HOTEL

rubber ring

sun lounger
deckchair

cliff
rock face
crag

The cliffs are...
craggy, rugged, jagged

Let's stop at the harbour for lunch.

Ouch! The crab bit my finger!

sailing boat

lifeguard

Shoo!

rock pool

shell

Look out! The sea's coming in.

fishing net

The sea can be...
rough
choppy
stormy
uneven

or...

calm
still
glassy
peaceful

Good throw!

The water...
ripples
laps
rolls

Beaches can be...
sandy
golden

or...

pebbly
stony
gravelly

squawk

Which sandcastle is better?

The tide...
comes in
rises

or...

goes out
falls

snorkel

The waves... swell, churn
foam, froth, crash

swim
bathe
dip

paddle, wade, splash

surfer

surfboard

25

Trees and flowers

Trees can have...

a trunk
branches
twigs
leaves
bark
roots
fruit
nuts
sap

They can be...

dense
leafy
green
lush

or...

sparse
bare
thin
bald

Trunks are...

strong
hardy
mighty

Branches can be...

bent, twisted, gnarled

or...

straight, smooth, solid

Vines...

wind, twine, coil

Bark can be...

tough
rough
knobbly

Seedlings...

grow
sprout
shoot up
develop
take root

CHEEP   CHIRP

bird's nest

Twigs are...

brittle
dry

They...

splinter
break

squirrel

acorns

Leaves...

fall

drop

tumble

hole
hollow

Some trees have...

needles
spines
thorns
cones

mushroom
toadstool
fungus

rabbit

SNIFF

worms

26

Flowers...
blossom
bloom

ear

petal

leaf

caterpillar
MUNCH

blade
of grass

Flowers
have...
a stem
petals
seeds
buds

They are...
pretty
bright
colourful
vibrant
sweet-smelling
fragrant

bzzzz

butterfly
FLAP
FLAP

bumble bee

Seeds...
spread
disperse
scatter

wilt
wither
shrivel

seed
head

Stems...
support
hold up
carry

stamen

pollen

droop, bend, bow, nod

Seed pods...
pop
burst
crack

Thistles
are...
prickly
spiky
sharp

shoot

bulb

bud

The undergrowth is...
wild, tangled, overgrown

soil
earth
mud

27

Where on Earth?

horizon

sand dunes

camel

Only a few hours to the next camp.

TRUDGE

expedition, journey, trek

The desert heat is...
blistering
sweltering
searing
fiery

cactus

palm trees

An oasis is...
cool, fresh, refreshing

lap

desert foxes

The land is...
dry   baked
sandy   bare
dusty   barren
scorched   parched

scorpion   SCUTTLE

spider's web

In the jungle, it's...
wet
damp
steamy
humid
muggy
sticky

PACAW!

DRIP

DRIP

creeper

Sap...
dribbles
trickles
oozes

hiss

Jungle animals...
buzz
screech
growl
hum
shriek
squawk

Jaguars...
prowl
stalk
hunt

Venus flytrap

SNAP

The forest floor is...
dark, gloomy, shady, shadowy

Playing sports

Who plays sports?
sportsperson
athlete
player
competitor
contestant

stretch
warm up
limber up

exercise
keep fit
work out

train
prepare
practise

coach

Ready, steady, GO!

rest
recover
relax

AAAAH

They can be...
fit
healthy
active
lively
energetic
sporty
acrobatic
agile
nimble
supple
flexible

ERK

lift
heave

Tug!

push

rope

pull
haul

Where do you play sports?
court
track
field
gym
pitch
ice rink
swimming pool
arena
stadium

WHEEEEE

BOING

bounce
spring

trampoline

hop

springboard

jump
leap

balance

Not far to go now!

puffing
panting
out of breath

jog

run
sprint
race

win
triumph
succeed

trophy

runner-up

winner
champion

race track

finish line

podium

medal

What do you need?

equipment
gear
kit

squash ball

tennis racket

boxing gloves

badminton racket

shuttlecock

baseball glove

goggles

ballet shoes

basketball

table tennis bat

tennis ball

ice hockey stick and puck

cricket bat

leg pads

knee pads

roller skates

weights

bicycle helmet

rugby ball

skis

climbing ropes

yoga mat

WHOOOOOOOOSH

throw
lob
fling

catch
grab
grasp
clutch

THWACK

hit
whack
strike
smash

TOWN TIGERS
CITY CUBS

scoreboard

DOH!

miss

Teams enter a...

tournament
match
game
competition
contest

supporters
fans
followers

WHOOP!

applaud
cheer

SCORE

GOAAAAAL!

shoot

goalkeeper

dive
lunge

They are...

competitive
determined
focused

kick, pass

They might...

win
draw
lose

dodge
weave

cheat
foul

Hey!
Play fairly.

dribble

tackle

referee

33

Telling a story

Choose an option from each box to tell a story.

WHEN?

Long, long ago...

Last Tuesday...

Once upon a time...

When I was a baby...

On an ordinary morning...

In the middle of the night...

At the beginning of time...

palace

castle

In Outer Space...

otherworldly
unearthly

space station

secret den

under the bed

WHERE?

faraway
distant
exotic
far-flung

desert island

familiar
everyday
normal
ordinary

school

A deep, dark forest...

magical
enchanted
fairytale

WHIR

CLANK

robot

vampire

mermaid

WHO?

princess

Fe, fi, fo, fum.

ARGH

giant

Grandma

I can fly!

unexpected
abnormal
out-of-the-ordinary

adventure
quest
mission

WHAT HAPPENS?

first of all
suddenly
instantly
all at once

ZAP

spell
enchantment
curse

splish

dab

invention
breakthrough
discovery

AWOOOO

werewolf

TADAH!

magician

astronaut

WHO DO THEY MEET?

spy

PUFF

dragon

genie

VROOM

getaway car

ID 126715001

secret identity

clue

WHAT WILL THEY NEED?

disguise

sidekick

spaceship

I told you to turn left!

problem
glitch
mishap

mix-up
muddle

I'm rich!

This isn't mine.

WHAT HAPPENS NEXT?

then
afterwards
finally

It was me!

surprise
shock
bombshell

plot
plan
heist

escape
getaway

happily ever after

WHAT HAPPENS IN THE END?

cliffhanger
homecoming
reunion
mystery solved

tragedy
sad ending

party
celebration
happy ending

35

Explorers are...
adventurous
intrepid
fearless

Inventors are...
intelligent
clever
brainy

X-ray goggles

Prepare to be saved, world!

Superheroes are...
mighty
powerful
invincible

Warriors are...
gifted
skilled
talented

They...
fight
battle
combat

Heroes...

Heroes can be...
brave
bold
courageous
plucky
kind
generous
good-hearted
magical
extraordinary
exceptional
remarkable
amazing
astounding

sword   armour

Sir Steve to the rescue!

shield

Knights are...
valiant
chivalrous
gallant

Princes and princesses are...
royal, regal, noble

wave

carriage

footman

Ways of speaking

say
tell
ask
answer
exclaim
mumble
whimper
snarl
babble
beg
sneer

boast
brag
gloat

shout
yell
bellow

cackle
croak
crow

moan
sigh
groan

whisper
murmur
mutter

BRAAAINS

Zombies are...
cursed
jinxed
doomed

Aliens...
attack, invade, strike

Take me to your leader.

Ghosts are...
spooky, ghoulish, eerie, paranormal

WOOOOOOOOOOOO

They...
haunt
torment
plague

RIP

Villains can be...
evil
wicked
nasty
cowardly
spineless
awful
fierce
vicious
grotesque
horrible
ghastly
gruesome

...and villains

Pirates are...
notorious
wanted
infamous

eye patch

treasure

wooden leg

They...
steal
loot
thieve

Lock him in the dungeon!

crown

Evil queens are...
ruthless
savage
brutal

GRRR

Monsters are...
frightening, terrifying, menacing

Ways of moving

march
stride
stroll
totter
lumber
lurch
saunter
trudge
stumble
shuffle
crawl

$

tiptoe
creep
sneak

stomp, tramp, stamp

swagger
parade
strut

limp
hobble
stagger

Puzzles and games

Find the opposites

Can you match each word to its opposite?

old

sour

pastel

tame

sweet

delighted

devastated

young

wild

bright

Missing words

One word in each sentence is missing.
Can you pick the best word to fill the gap?

1. I'm the .... monster in the land.

fiercest
cutest
cleanest

2. This curry is too ....!

spicy
scary
sporty

3. Yippee, we .... the match.

lost
won
threw

4. We love .... in the countryside.

driving
hiking
scrubbing

5. I've hurt my ....

shoulder
hand
leg

6. Hey! Stop being so ....

shy
greedy
friendly

7. My hair is ....

curly
chatty
salty

8. We're all in the ....

car
coach
plane

Word match

Which word in the list below could you use instead?

angry

hungry
furious
glad

enormous

careful
narrow
huge

creep

sneak
sprint
shout

sporty

athletic
lazy
sparkly

sleepy

cool
grey
dozy

Mixed-up stories

These two stories have been mixed up. Can you put them in the right order?

Spotting game

Look back through the book to find the answers to these questions.

1. Can you find us on holiday?

2. Shopping is BORING. Can you find me playing a game in the snow?

3. Can you spot me relaxing on my deckchair on two pages?

4. Wahoo! Can you spot us zooming on two different pages?

5. Where's our school? Can you find it?

6. Can you find me eating something sour?

7. How many times can you spot us in the book?

Spotting game
1. page 25
2. page 29
3. pages 25 and 28
4. pages 6 and 24
5. page 22
6. page 20
7. four times: on pages 2, 7, 9 and 22

Mixed-up stories
1, 4, 3, 2.
A, D, B, C.

Word match
angry - furious
enormous - huge
creep - sneak
sporty - athletic
sleepy - dozy

Missing words
1. fiercest
2. spicy
3. won
4. hiking
5. leg
6. greedy
7. curly
8. car.

Find the opposites
old - young
pastel - bright
sweet - sour
devastated - delighted
wild - tame

USBORNE QUICKLINKS

For links to websites with word games and activities, go to the Usborne Quicklinks website at **www.usborne.com/quicklinks** and type in the title of this book.

We recommend that children are supervised while on the internet.

MANAGING EDITOR: Ruth Brocklehurst   MANAGING DESIGNER: Nickey Butler   LITERACY CONSULTANT: Kerenza Ghosh

First published in 2017 by Usborne Publishing Ltd., 83-85 Saffron Hill, London, EC1N 8RT, England. www.usborne.com Copyright © 2017 Usborne Publishing Ltd.